Original title:
Tying the Path Together

Copyright © 2025 Creative Arts Management OÜ
All rights reserved.

Author: Ryan Sterling
ISBN HARDBACK: 978-1-80586-192-8
ISBN PAPERBACK: 978-1-80586-664-0

Converging Roads

Two lanes merge in a quirky twist,
Where signposts dance, none can resist.
A squirrel holds the traffic light,
Bouncing through the day so bright.

Drivers laugh with coffee spills,
As GPS plays mischievous thrills.
Left or right? A game of chance,
Mismatched shoes in a silly dance.

The Dance of Togetherness

A pair of socks begin to waltz,
One's polka dots, the other vaults.
In the kitchen, spoons hold a show,
While forks debate where they should go.

The butter churns, giving a cheer,
As eggs jiggle, causing a leer.
Whisking mischief into the night,
Everything's grooving, oh what a sight!

Harmonized Horizons

Clouds and sun play peekaboo,
While birds debate the best view.
One flies left, another right,
Chasing rainbows, what a sight!

Mountains giggle at valley jokes,
While rivers burst with silly strokes.
Together they float in giggly glee,
Creating a scene of jubilee.

Destiny's Footprints

Two shoes meet on a path so wide,
One's a runner, the other's a slide.
They chat about the places they've been,
In puddles of laughter, they've always been seen.

As they prance through mud, there's a splash,
One shoe slips, oh what a crash!
Together they journey, side by side,
With each silly stumble, they take their stride.

United in Voyage

On a boat made of marshmallows,
We sailed through chocolate streams.
The seagulls wore sunglasses,
As we all chased our dreams.

With a map drawn in crayon,
We laughed at our silly plight.
Navigating through jellyfish,
In a sea of pure delight.

The captain was a raccoon,
Who swabbed the deck with style.
He pointed to the starfish,
And danced around for a while.

We toasted with soda pop,
To all the friends we'd made,
On this bizarre adventure,
Where laughter never fades.

The Nexus of Dreams

In a world of floating teacups,
We swirled beneath candy skies.
A frog in a tuxedo spoke,
With wisdom that made us sighs.

We played tag with the rainbows,
As colors began to blend.
Tickling clouds with giggles,
Where laughter knows no end.

A snail served us spaghetti,
On a plate of golden glow.
Every bite was an adventure,
With a sauce like a rainbow.

As night fell on our journey,
Stars began to hum and sing.
In this nexus of our dreams,
We danced around like spring.

Paths Intertwined

Two squirrels roamed the forest,
Plotting their acorn heist.
They hopped from branch to branch,
In a world of nutty yeast.

A racetrack made of gumdrops,
Became their racing ground.
With marshmallow pit stops,
Laughter echoed all around.

They tangled in each other,
In a game of hide and seek.
Fell into berry bushes,
With cheeks all rosy pink.

Together in their antics,
No challenge was too great.
In the paths that intertwined,
They found a friendship fate.

In the Space Between

In the space between the raindrops,
We danced with joyful glee.
Hopping on fluffy puddles,
As the clouds tried to flee.

A cat with a magic hat,
Pulled out a fish on a string.
We laughed till our stomachs hurt,
In this silly, wondrous fling.

Time was but a rubber band,
Stretching far and wide.
In the space where we connected,
Worries tried to hide.

With giggles like confetti,
Falling from skies of dreams,
We found joy in the fractures,
And splashed through silly streams.

Stitching Memories

In a quilt of quirks, we sew,
Each patch a tale, don't you know?
A button here, a snip right there,
Laughter spills beyond repair.

We stitch on Sundays, quite the sight,
With threads of joy, we take delight.
Unruly patterns come undone,
Yet somehow, we still have our fun.

Grandma's sweater—what a mess!
A knitted beast, but who would guess?
With tangled yarn and bits of fluff,
We giggle, claiming it's enough.

Patchwork hearts, we still believe,
In each odd theme we now conceive.
From mismatched socks to jumbled dreams,
Together, we're a wacky team.

The Nexus of Existence

In a world where socks do flee,
And every shoe hides where it may be.
We dance around in silly loops,
Chasing ducks and baked-up scoops.

A rubber chicken in my hand,
Is that a joke, or just a stand?
With cosmic giggles echoing wide,
Life's punchlines are the best to ride.

Einstein's hair, a wild affair,
And gravity? It trips us where!
With laughter soaring like a kite,
We navigate this comic flight.

Creating chaos, oh what fun,
With every step, a race we run.
As time loops back like silly strings,
We marvel at the joy it brings.

Winding Ribbons of Fate

With ribbons bright, we twist and twirl,
Like tangled hair in a whirl.
Each step we take, a quirky dance,
A chance encounter, a funny glance.

Serendipity tied in bows,
From buttered toast to garden hose.
We giggle at the leaps we make,
As fortune smiles on our mistake.

A cat that sneezes, jumps at air,
A rubber band that's gone somewhere.
We chase our tails in merry rounds,
While laughter echoes, joy abounds.

So hold on tight to silly threads,
Through winding paths, let laughter spreads.
For in this yarn of life we weave,
There's endless joy, just believe.

Synchronized Horizons

In sunbeam meetings, we collide,
With coffee cups and hearts full wide.
A misstep here, a hiccup there,
In synchronized chaos, we share.

We mimic birds, all in a row,
Chasing clouds, with "Oops!" and "Whoa!"
In moments where we find our groove,
Life's funny dance, we always move.

With wobbly boats on a lake,
We paddle hard for laughter's sake.
Leaving ripples, jokes afloat,
In the chuckles we all wrote.

So here's to life—a comical scene,
With sunsets painted in shades of green.
Together we stride, silly and bright,
Creating smiles, our shared delight.

Uniting the Footprints

In a land where shoes were lost,
Socks wandered off at their own cost.
A flip-flop met a stiletto there,
Danced in circles, without a care.

Gumboots laughed at sandals' plight,
While bunny slippers twirled at night.
Each footprint formed a silly plot,
Tails of laughter shared on the spot.

Sneakers raced with clogs in tow,
Through muddy puddles, they did flow.
Their paths entwined in much delight,
A wobbly race, oh what a sight!

As the sun began to set,
A pirate's boot of sunken debt,
Joined hands with crocs, oh what a scheme,
To find their way back to the dream.

Harmonies in Motion

A waltz began with shoes so bright,
Rubber soles and heels took flight.
Each step a note, a funky beat,
In grand ballet, they found their feat.

Laces tangled in a jig,
Socks and sandals felt so big.
As flip-flops hummed a summer tune,
Slippers spun under the moon.

Heels strutted with a trusty cap,
In sync they made a comic map.
Across the lawn, a prancing spree,
Achieving chaos joyfully!

As shoes departed from the dance,
Each took the stage to find romance.
With giggles floating on the breeze,
They formed a band, the best of keys!

Web of Wanderings

Once a sneaker lost its pair,
Got tangled in a curious snare.
A wooly sock joined for the fun,
Together they would surely run.

The shoelace spun like a dancer,
Found a pebble, its only enhancer.
The forest stirred with giggles loud,
As boots and slippers formed a crowd.

Together they spun a silly tale,
Of wandering feet that never fail.
Through puddles deep and grassy knolls,
They chased the sun with happy souls.

Ultimately, they claimed their time,
Each mismatched shoe danced in rhyme.
With laughter echoing in the glen,
They vowed to meet as friends again!

Boundless Journeys

A sock hopped on a lurking shoe,
Searching for adventures new.
It traded fluff for a small ride,
On a flip-flop's back, they cried.

Through tangled grass and nearby streams,
They wove together all their dreams.
A pancake flip led to a race,
Where runners laughed and shared their space.

As sneakers raced down endless trails,
Each step echoed of joyful tales.
A chirpy bird invited them near,
Brought laughter echoing in the cheer.

Finally, they collapsed in glee,
Formed a pillow, flat as can be.
Journey's end, but joy's not shy,
Together they could always fly.

Interlacing Destinies

Two socks in a dryer spin around,
One claimed the throne, the other, a hound.
They teamed up in laughter, a fuzzy parade,
Chasing dust bunnies, in silliness swayed.

An ant on a mission, a snail creeping slow,
Joined forces for snacks, both craving a show.
With crumbs as their compass, they tread through the crumbs,
In their wacky alliance, adventure becomes!

A giraffe and a turtle, an odd pair indeed,
Sought a tall tree for a sumptuous feed.
"Just lift me up high!", the turtle did yell,
With a neck-stretching wish, they both rang the bell.

Together they wobbled, their hearts full of cheer,
Beneath the wide sky, shared snacks far and near.
With giggles abundant, their friendship imparted,
In the fabric of fate, they both felt lighthearted.

Bridges Over Time

A beaver and otter, they built quite the dream,
With logs and with laughter, they crafted a scheme.
Each plank that was laid was a joke in disguise,
While laughing at splashes, they reached for the skies.

As seasons rolled on, the bridge told a tale,
Of squirrels who would dance, without fear of a fail.
With nuts flying past, they'd all kick up their feet,
In a silly ballet, they made laughter repeat.

The river below whispered secrets of cheer,
As frogs in tuxedos croaked songs to their ear.
With giggles and splashes, the party would flow,
"You're toe-tapping too? Just go with the flow!"

At dusk they'd all gather, with stars shining bright,
Recalling wild escapades under moonlight.
Two friends turned to family, a bridge made of bliss,
In the dance of their tales, how could one resist?

When Paths Converge

A chicken with dreams of a big-time parade,
Met a duck on a quest with a grand serenade.
Together they waddled, a curious pair,
With feathers all fluffed, strutting flair everywhere.

At corners they stumbled, with giggles and flaps,
Swapping wild tales while plotting their laps.
They challenged the winds with each gusty hello,
As /bawk-bawks/ echoed, their bond began to grow.

Through puddles of mischief, they danced with delight,
With goofy adventures, they'd shine through the night.
They'd take silly selfies, look what they achieved,
In this wacky race, their friendship believed.

At a fork in the road, they skipped, no regret,
With a cluck and a quack, their fates would be met.
With feathers entwined, their giggles they'd urge,
In this quirky adventure, together they'd surge.

Echoes of Shared Direction

A wise old owl met a young, spry fox,
Who claimed to know secrets about the big clocks.
"Let's travel through time, with giggles and cheers,
And harvest some laughter through all of the years!"

With feathers and fur, they dived into dreams,
Glimpsing the past with its whimsical schemes.
A dance with the daisies, a race with the breeze,
They twirled through the ages with absolute ease.

From cavemen in caves to robots in space,
With every wild twist, they laughed and embraced.
They shared silly stories, from future to past,
In the echoes of time, their friendships would last.

So here's to the journeys that laughter does spark,
With wise owls and foxes, embracing the dark.
For in every adventure that matters most dear,
Are the giggles and chuckles that keep us all near.

Echoes Through Seasons

When winter snowflakes start to fall,
The children giggle, make a snowball.
They toss it high, it flies away,
Landing right on Grandma's tray.

In spring, the flowers start to bloom,
Kids wear hats that spell "Vroom Vroom!"
A bee buzzes loud, they all take flight,
Chasing it off in sheer delight.

Summer brings a cheerful sun,
Ice cream cones, oh what fun!
But sticky fingers tell the tale,
Of melting treats that won't prevail.

Autumn leaves, they start to swirl,
Dancing kids in a leaf whirl.
With pumpkins round, they carve a laugh,
Scaring neighbors on their path.

The Journey of Many

Two friends set off with snacks in hand,
On a grand trip across the land.
They took a wrong turn at the creek,
Found a cow that simply squeaked.

They laughed and danced around the field,
While the lazy cow refused to yield.
"Climb on up!" one shouted with glee,
Off they went, just to see!

With sandwiches stuck to their hair,
They waved to squirrels, oh what a pair!
But soon their feet began to ache,
So they found a pond for a snack break.

The journey's strange, with twists and bends,
But every laugh, the fun extends.
Through mishaps shared, they build a tale,
Of cows, and snacks, and leaves that sail.

Weaving Whispers in the Wind

The breeze flutters through the trees,
Whispers secrets like a tease.
It tickles leaves and makes them sway,
As squirrels begin to join the play.

A kite soars high, with colors bold,
Chasing stories that remain untold.
But tangled strings in a laughing whirl,
Bring kites and kids into a twirl.

The wind confesses tales at dusk,
Of naughty cats and stinky musk.
Each gust a giggle, each breeze a sigh,
As shadows dance and fireflies fly.

So let's all leap, embrace the fun,
With every twirl and every run.
For life's a game of twists and bends,
A joyful tale that never ends.

Unity in Motion

In a line we hop, in a line we skip,
With silly hats and a funny lip.
Together we dance, all hand in hand,
Creating a scene that's quite unplanned.

While balancing books on our heads,
And laughing loud, like silly sleds.
"Watch your step!" one cries in a fit,
But we just grin and dance a bit.

At every corner, we spin around,
Twirling off into the ground.
With laughter bursting, joy abounds,
In every step, our friendship found.

So come along, let's roll and sway,
In unity's dance, we laugh and play.
With hearts so light, and spirits bright,
Together we shine, 'til the night.

Across the Fabric of Time

In socks that vanish, time does flee,
My left foot's lonely, where could it be?
Ticking clocks play hide and seek,
Napping minutes, oh so meek.

Past and present, what a mess,
Yesterday's lunch, I can't confess.
Wearing mismatched shoes on my stroll,
Fashion icons? Not quite my goal.

Watch the seconds do the dance,
Eternity laughs at my glance.
Spin around, trip on fate's shoe,
What's a little time warp to you?

Each moment's thread a charming joke,
Laughter stitched in every poke.
Time's a fabric, torn and fun,
Wobbly stitches, still we run.

Uniting Starlit Trails

Under stars with wobbly glow,
Moonlit mischief, on we go.
Tripping over dreamy sights,
Giggling at those silly flights.

Navigating through the night,
Falling over thoughts in flight.
Cosmic rubber bands at play,
Snap and bounce the night away.

Twinkling tales from far-off lands,
Tangled giggles, sticky hands.
Navigators of the silly skies,
With shooting stars as our surprise.

Our paths merge with starry grace,
Laughter found in every space.
Here we are, just having fun,
Underneath the cosmic run.

The Threads We Trace

In yarns of joy, we weave our day,
Loop-de-loop, come what may.
A cat jumps in, what a sight,
Knitting chaos, pure delight.

Colors clash, patterns collide,
My scarf looks like it needs a guide.
With pom-poms dancing here and there,
Crafting giggles in the air.

Purl a stitch, then drop the ball,
One big tangle, can't recall.
We count our stitches, one, two, three,
Laughter's the thread that sets us free.

In every knot, a tale unfolds,
Weaving friendship; it never gets old.
With every loop, we share the glee,
Crafting moments, just you and me.

Bridges of Connection

Building bridges, oh what fun,
Over puddles, we do run.
Splashes here, a jump, a cheer,
Wiggly paths, we have no fear.

With rubber ducks and paper planes,
We connect through joyful lanes.
Pretend to cross the highest hills,
With silly walks that give us thrills.

Duct tape bridges span so wide,
Wobbly laughs, we take in stride.
Connected hearts in every beat,
A friendship built that can't be beat.

Laughter echoes through each space,
In every hop, we leave a trace.
Here we stand, side by side,
Bridges built on joy and pride.

Unfolding the Journey

A cat in a hat, oh what a sight,
With shoes on his paws, he's ready to fight.
He dances and prances, a comical show,
Chasing his tail, to and fro so slow.

A squirrel on a skateboard, zooming past,
Spreading such joy, making moments last.
They wave to the snail, who's taking his time,
Singing a song, oh so out of rhyme.

One Step at a Time

Step by step, a chicken does strut,
In oversized shoes, oh what a nut!
He trips on a worm, who laughs out loud,
Then joins in the dance, feeling quite proud.

A frog in a top hat leaps with flair,
Hopping on marshmallows, light as air.
Together they waddle, a clumsy parade,
Each wobble and tumble a glorious escapade.

Converging Echoes

An echo of giggles bounces around,
A dog with a pogo stick leaps off the ground.
He barks at the moon, with a wink and a paw,
As the stars join the fun, in a cosmic awe.

A duo of ducks take flight in a spin,
Quacking up chaos, a whimsical din.
They land on a trampoline, bouncing with cheer,
Creating a puddle of laughter, oh dear!

A Tapestry of Moments

A patchwork of antics, a jester's delight,
A llama in sunglasses, basking in light.
With a twist and a turn, he struts with style,
While a rabbit in bowties applauds with a smile.

A parade of oddballs, a carnival crew,
The grape in a tutu, the apple in blue.
Each moment a stitch in this fabric of fun,
Where laughter and joy are forever spun.

Boundless Roads Intersect

Down the wobbly road, a bear on a bike,
Pedals turning slowly, oh what a hike!
He wobbles and giggles, trying to steer,
As a raccoon in goggles gives a loud cheer.

In fields where the daisies toss confetti,
A parade of frogs stage a dance, quite petty.
With flippers and hats, they twirl with glee,
Creating a ruckus, as silly as can be.

An Entwined Odyssey

In a world where paths collide,
Socks and sandals take a ride.
Bicycles and skateboards race,
While tumbleweeds bring up the pace.

A squirrel steals a sandwich treat,
While joggers dodge the dancing feet.
The mailman's hat flies high and wide,
He laughs as puppies try to hide.

A cat on a leash leads the way,
Chasing pigeons who wish to play.
A runner trips on his own shoe laces,
And bursts out laughing in funny faces.

When paths entwine like tangled vines,
Expect the unexpected to take its signs.
In mishaps, giggles echo strong,
Together we march; let's sing along!

Intersections of Time

At noon, the clock starts spinning round,
And crossing signs are upside down.
A turtle races an old man's stroll,
While time forgets its very goal.

The pigeons plot a sneaky coup,
As tourists step in a gooey stew.
A child shouts, "Look! An alien!"
Turns out it's just a guy with a pen.

A lady drops her ice cream cone,
As a dog claims it as his own.
Laughter bubbles up like fizzy drink,
In moments of chaos, we often think.

The sun and moon do a silly dance,
As mismatched socks get a second chance.
With laughter echoing through the street,
Our stories weave in jumbled feet.

Unity in the Journey

A marching band of ants in line,
Carrying crumbs, feeling so fine.
They trip over a soda can,
Becoming dancers in a little jam.

The butterfly trips on a flower's petal,
While bees compete in a buzz-off medal.
The sun winks down on all the fun,
As shadows play and birds all run.

Picnics blend with football games,
As ice cream melts and no one blames.
A cat chases its tail in delight,
While squirrels debate the best flight.

In this circus of moments shared,
Unexpected chaos, but no one's scared.
Together we tumble, we laugh and sway,
Unity shines in its own quirky way.

The Conjoined Trail

Two socks lost in a dryer's lure,
Dance around to a rhythm unsure.
A sandwich slides off the picnic spread,
While ants conspire to steal the bread.

A noodle slipped off the plate so sly,
Lands on a dog who thinks it can fly.
The juggler drops three balls on a frown,
As laughter erupts, he takes a bow down.

In a world of chaos, blissfully torn,
The sun tickles clouds, as laughter is born.
A bicycle tire spins out of control,
While a kid claims, "I'm a rock and roll!"

Winding together our misfit trails,
We find joy in the oddest tales.
Embracing the laughter, we stand and cheer,
For every goofy moment that brings us near.

Shared Steps Under Stars

In cosmic dance, we trip and twirl,
With alien socks, we twist and whirl.
Our shoes untie, they laugh and squeak,
A starry night, our knees go weak.

We stumble past a glowing hare,
He rolls his eyes, says, "Not a care!"
We share a laugh, then take a leap,
To count the stars, a bond so deep.

Under these lights, we try to sing,
But oh dear me, we lost a string!
Our off-key chorus fills the air,
As comets blush and wink, beware!

The sky's our guide, so wild and bright,
With meteor trails in the moonlit night.
Each jumbled step, a joyful ride,
Together we hop, in glee, we glide.

Crossing Together

With every leap across the brook,
We dodged the splash, that was the hook.
A frog leaped high, we missed our aim,
Now soggy socks are part of the game.

Through muddy trails and hints of glue,
We find a snail, our trusty crew.
He gives a nod, we cheer him on,
In this wild race, we're never gone!

At every turn, the trees all sway,
They chuckle loud, come join the fray!
With every twist, a giggle so bright,
Our journey's filled with pure delight.

Together we roam, arms open wide,
In this odd world, we're side by side.
Every step adds laughter, oh what fun,
As we cross together, joy has begun!

The Bonds of Exploration

With backpacks full of snacks galore,
We trek through jungles, always more.
A cheeky monkey steals a bite,
We yell, 'Hey there! That's not polite!'

Our maps are scribbles, paths are unclear,
Yet every turn, we have no fear.
A compass laughs, spins in delight,
We're lost again, but it feels just right.

In caves so dark, we tell our tales,
Of epic fails and fishy trails.
A bat flies by to join our fun,
In this wild game, we've already won!

Each step we take, a story unfolds,
In giggles and grins, the adventure molds.
We roam this world, our spirits take flight,
United in joy, our hearts feel light.

We Are the Journey

In mismatched shoes, we start to roam,
From city lights to fields of foam.
Each step we take, a hop and skip,
With giggling fits, we'll never trip!

We chase the clouds, they race so fast,
With silly faces, we'll hold our blast.
A breeze throws curls, oh what a sight,
We laugh so hard, it feels just right.

Through puddles deep, we leap with glee,
Like dancing dolphins at sea, oh whee!
With every splash, a love so bright,
Together we shine, a sparkling light.

Exploring together, lost and found,
On this wild trail, joy's all around.
In every mishap, we find our tune,
For we are the journey, in sun and moon.

A Junction of Souls

At the crosswalk, we pause and grin,
Sidewalk chalk dreams, where to begin?
Silly hat tricks and mismatched shoes,
Laughter erupts, it's the silliest views.

Traffic lights dance like they know the beat,
Waving at strangers, a friendly greet.
Bumping into life's quirky design,
We shrug our shoulders, say, "It's just fine!"

Pigeons coo as they strut in a line,
Chasing crumbs like they hit the divine.
In a crowded café, we share our tales,
Espresso shots chased by giggling gales.

So when we meet at this jolly place,
With grins wide enough to fill the space,
Let's raise our cups to these funny twists,
In the junction of souls, nothing's amiss!

Shared Horizons

On the horizon, with bright balloons,
We chase sunsets and jabber like loons.
Waltzing with shadows, we trip and sway,
Making up songs as we go on our way.

Kites in the air, they wave and dive,
Spinning yarns of the times we feel alive.
With each string we pull, laughter takes hold,
In shared horizons, memories unfold.

Searching for treasure in the local park,
Finding funny hats, aiming to spark.
Dancing on benches, we cheer and shout,
In this odd adventure, there's never a doubt.

So let's draw maps with our crayon hearts,
Celebrating journeys and whimsical parts.
With every giggle, our spirits expand,
We paint our world, hand in hand.

Fusion of Footsteps

As we stumble on this crazy road,
Our shoes make music with a funny ode.
Every step a giggle, every sway a cheer,
Together we dance, no worries here.

We trip on pebbles, we laugh till we cry,
Side by side under the cotton candy sky.
With silly gestures, we break out in song,
In the fusion of footsteps, we can't go wrong.

Lost in the moment, our worries dissolve,
Finding joy in chaos, we love to evolve.
Chasing the wind, where wildflowers bloom,
In this comical chase, we're free like a plume.

So let's waddle forth, with rhythm and rhyme,
Making merriment out of no time.
With every clumsy twist, our laughter ignites,
Creating magic in our shared flights.

The Confluence of Journeys

Where roads intersect, we find a delight,
Like two lost socks finding their light.
With maps upside down, we search for the fun,
In this quirky dance, we've already won.

Sprinkling giggles like confetti around,
Our paths intertwine, a whimsical sound.
Hiccups and snorts in a shared car ride,
As we embrace the wacky, let's enjoy the slide.

At junctions of joy, we skip and we shout,
With every detour, we learn what it's about.
Finding adventure where none was intended,
In the confluence of journeys, life's splendidly blended.

So here's to our stories, both silly and bold,
In laughter's warm arms, may we never grow old.
With each twist and turn, let's make our mark,
In this grand journey, forever we'll spark.

Paths Illuminated

Bouncing along in mismatched shoes,
We trip on laughter, no way to lose.
Hopping over puddles, splashing bright,
Chasing down rainbows, what a sight!

With every turn, we chance a spin,
Dodging the squirrels, they tease and grin.
Under the sun, our shadows play,
Who knew walking could be this way!

A map of giggles, a compass of cheer,
We follow the twists that bring us near.
No destination, just joy in our strides,
Together we march where fun abides!

Through bushes and branches, we weave along,
Singing a silly, nonsensical song.
With a hop and a skip, we'll find our fate,
Every step away, we dance, we prate!

The Unity of Travels

Luggage in tow, we stumble and sway,
Mixing our snacks in a humorous fray.
Who packed the pickles? What's this I find?
Journey's more fun when you're unconfined!

With maps that confuse and directions that spin,
We wander in circles, let the laughter begin.
Each wrong turn leads to a tale anew,
Like the time you thought a cow was a clue!

As the sun sets low, we sit for a bite,
Sharing stories and snacks under starlight.
We toast with our sodas, as giggles arise,
In this unity travel, it's no surprise!

So let's lose our way, and maybe our minds,
For the best of adventures are the most unrefined.
With each silly mishap, we grow closer still,
Crammed in the backseat; it's a comedy thrill!

Footprints Entwined

In the sand we walk, our steps intertwine,
Leaving a sketch of a dance, oh so fine.
The crabs wave hello as we parade by,
Even the seagulls chuckle and fly!

With jokes tossed like shells, we laugh and complain,
Every misstep is cause for champagne.
Where sunscreen was missed, we wear stripes of red,
Sandy sandwiches are enough to have fed!

Through twisting paths of beach and of shore,
We skip past the hassle, searching for more.
Building a fortress with buckets and spades,
You guard with a seagull; this friendship won't fade!

As the tide moves in, we jump in retreat,
Splashing like fools in our rubbery feet.
With laughter echoing under the sun,
These footprints we leave, forever fun!

Odyssey of Us

In our cart of dreams, we roll down the lane,
Waving to neighbors, who think we're insane.
Mixing up gadgets, each one a surprise,
Like the time you tried to bike with your thighs!

The road stretches onward, we shout out our tales,
Of highway adventures and misdelivered mails.
With snacks in our laps and a song in our heart,
We're conquerors of chaos, each leg a new part!

Bumpy rides equal laughter, that's how we roll,
With puns that are terrible, fulfilling our goal.
To savor the silly, to cherish the fun,
In this odyssey shared, we've already won!

So here's to the journeys, however they weave,
With memories made that we won't believe.
Through ups and downs, we're a riotous crew,
Adventure is grand, especially with you!

Merging Footprints

Two left feet and one right shoe,
We dance through mud, who knew?
Socks all soggy, laughter flows,
Following footprints, where it goes!

A clown slipped on a banana peel,
His antics made the asphalt reel.
We zigzagged down the busy street,
Chasing giggles, what a feat!

In puddles deep, we splash and play,
Skipping stones on a sunny day.
With every leap, we make a mark,
Each jump sending us into the park!

Life's a race with silly shoes,
Pace unsteady, but we choose.
With laughter loud, we find our way,
In jumbled steps, we seize the day!

Chords of Experience

A tuba note on a sunny morn,
With guitar strings that stretch and yawn.
We pluck a laugh from the bright air,
In silly tuneful disrepair!

The banjo twangs, it sounds so wrong,
But it hums a laugh, we sing along.
Each note a bump, each chord a smile,
Making music, mile by mile!

Is that a kazoo in the mix?
It squeaks and squawks, gives us fits.
With every blunder, the rhythm stays,
Creating joy in wacky ways!

In this orchestra, we find our beat,
With instruments made of leftover treats.
As laughter weaves through our delight,
We play our hearts out, day and night!

The Harmony of Passage

On a bicycle built for two,
We pedal fast, who knew?
A wobbly ride down the lane,
With silly hats—it's never plain!

The cartwheeling dog runs up ahead,
Chasing birds, and crumbs of bread.
We steer and giggle, take a chance,
In this joyful, bumpy dance!

Under the sun, we race the breeze,
With squeaky wheels and wobbly knees.
Friends on a journey, can't be late,
We'll conquer every twist of fate!

Our laughter echoes down the roads,
As we juggle life, with our loads.
In harmony, we take each stride,
Together, we'll enjoy the ride!

Knotted Stories

A shoelace tangled, what a sight,
Twisted tales that feel just right.
With every knot, a giggling sigh,
As stories spun, flutter and fly!

Grandpa's tales with a twisty end,
A flying cat? That's quite the friend!
Each yarn we weave, just makes us grin,
Through knotted threads, we always win!

Under the stars, we gather 'round,
With laughter shared and joys abound.
The night unfolds, adventures grow,
In tangled tales, our spirits glow!

So lend an ear to whispered dreams,
And laugh at life's odd little schemes.
For in our hearts, the stories spin,
Knotted together, we begin!

The Dance of Directions

In the land of lost umbrellas,
Left feet lead right shoes astray,
Maps flip like fish in puddles,
And GPS is on holiday.

Rabbits hop while turtles race,
With signs that twist and wiggle,
A penguin guides the errant pace,
As laughter bursts in a giggle.

Roundabouts spin like disco balls,
While squirrels throw acorn parties,
I ask directions, hear the calls,
And dance with strangers, feeling farty.

So if you trip while on the way,
Embrace the blunders, that's the key,
In this wild waltz, we laugh and sway,
Together, we roam—let's just be free.

Woven Threads of Journey

Each day's a stitch, both bright and bold,
Gathering tales like granny's quilt,
From morning coffee, silly and cold,
To laughing over the facts we wilt.

Eagles soar while turtles plod,
In cosmic yarns where dreams align,
The universe gives an honest nod,
To mishaps woven into design.

A stray cat yawns, times it right,
As we juggle snacks with flair and flair,
We hand out devil-may-care delight,
While fabric of life hangs in mid-air.

So grab a slice, recline in cheer,
Embrace the knots and twists that come,
For every quirk we hold dear,
Is the thread that makes life fun!

Celestial Crossroads

Stars twinkle in a clueless sky,
While roads meet like jigsaw pieces,
We'll chase the moon, let out a sigh,
With every turn, our laughter increases.

A cow gives directions, wild and free,
Holding a map with a confused tail,
Are we lost, or just meant to be?
As we dance in circles, leaving a trail.

Martians giggle at our Earthly ways,
While time flies on a rubber band,
In every starlit, foolish phase,
We find our footing in the sand.

So here we stand, at this bright crossroad,
With cosmic humor in our sight,
Every twist, a quirky code,
Guiding us through the starry night.

The Fabric of Our Steps

In socks that do not match, we prance,
As mischief weaves through every stride,
Life's a merry, clumsy dance,
With tangled threads that we take in stride.

A dog drags me down the lane,
Chasing after a butterfly bold,
Each step a giggle, not in vain,
With stories of mischief yet untold.

Pigeons seem to join our spree,
As we trip on the tiles below,
And weave our tales with flair and glee,
Painting the pavement with wild flow.

So grab a thread, come join the fun,
In this fabric of glee, let's connect,
For every stumble, every run,
Makes this journey truly perfect!

Weaving the Road Ahead

As we skip along the road,
With a map of silly codes.
Each step a dance, a little twirl,
With laughter in a joyful swirl.

We stitch together every laugh,
A patchwork made of our own gaffs.
Each bump and twist a punchline bright,
Weaving smiles into the night.

Tapestry of Togetherness

We're threads of colors, bright and bold,
Knots and tangles, stories told.
Each giggle's a stitch, each chuckle a seam,
Creating a quilt of silly dreams.

With mischief woven in every row,
We pull at strings, let the laughter flow.
In this crazy weave, we find our way,
Sewing memories in a bright array.

Links Between the Lines

In a world where winks are drawn,
We connect with giggles at dawn.
Every pun a link, strong and tight,
  Balancing joy, left and right.

Our jokes are vines that twist and twine,
  Growing in rhythm, so divine.
In each funny tale, we find the way,
Connecting smiles, come what may.

The Ties that Bind Us

Giggling ropes we weave and spin,
Pulling each other, no way to pin.
With every laugh, a knot we make,
A friendship born from each mistake.

Twisted paths, but oh so bright,
Guiding us through day and night.
With humor as our guiding star,
There's no limit to how far.

Intricate Moves

In the dance of life we sway,
With feet that sometimes quite betray.
A left, then right, we trip and spin,
Laughter erupts, let the fun begin!

Our friends all join in the show,
With moves that make the rhythm flow.
They twirl and stumble, a hilarious sight,
As we laugh through day and into the night.

The music plays, the steps get bold,
Wondering who will be the first to fold.
Yet amidst the chaos, joy is found,
In every slip, we're joyfully bound!

So let's keep dancing, let's not grow shy,
Each twist and turn, oh me, oh my!
With every bobble, we muster glee,
In this twisted jig, we dance so free!

The Unity of Unfolding

We gather here for a grand parade,
With mismatched socks and lemonade.
Our outfits clash in crazy ways,
Yet unity blooms in the silly displays!

As floats roll by with laughter loud,
The sight of clowns makes us proud.
Balloons collide, a colorful mess,
We giggle and snort, we couldn't care less.

Together we prance, like one big sock,
A tumbling mass of joy that can't be locked.
Each silly face we paint with cheer,
As the parade unfolds, we all appear!

So let's continue this wild delight,
With each silly moment, the world feels right.
An oddball procession, where chaos gives way,
To joy that shines brighter than sun's perfect ray!

Roads of Resonance

On this winding road, we trip and fall,
With every giggle, we answer the call.
Sidewalks swerve like a flowing stream,
As we dance through life, a recurring dream!

From silly hats to mismatched shoes,
Echoes of laughter, that's how we choose.
Roads diverge, yet still we roam,
Together we wander, forever our home!

A hop, a skip, oh look, I missed,
Every slight stumble just can't be skipped.
Voices of joy drift through the air,
Each shared moment, a whimsical flair!

So let's take this road, with all its turns,
A journey so bright, our laughter returns.
With every misstep, oh what a thrill,
As we wander together, we find our will!

The Weave of Every Step

In the fabric of life, we stitch our dreams,
With patchwork patterns and silly schemes.
Each step we take, a stitch that binds,
In this ragtag quilt, joy is the finds!

Threads of color go in and out,
Creating chaos, that's what it's about.
With every goofy twist and twirl,
We brighten up our whirling world!

So pass the needle, let's mend this thread,
With snickers and chuckles, nothing to dread.
Every loop and knot, we weave with grace,
Each funny moment leaves us in lace!

Together we craft this tapestry bright,
In the quilt of our lives, laughter takes flight.
With every fiber, our fun will stay,
As we stitch memories, come what may!

The Symphony of Trails

Bouncing in boots like a kangaroo,
Each step a note in this lively stew.
With squirrels as conductors, we leap and twirl,
Nature's orchestra in a giggly whirl.

A snail in a tux, what a sight to see!
He shrugs off the race, just as slow as can be.
While birds harmonize with the sweetest of calls,
The bushes join in, as if they have balls.

We zig and we zag, trying to keep pace,
But trip on a root – oh, what a disgrace!
Yet laughter erupts, as we brush off the dirt,
In this muddy ballet, we frolic and flirt.

So here's to the trails, with their winks and their grins,
Every stumble and giggle, as nature begins.
Let's dance with the wild, sing loud and be free,
In this symphony of trails, it's just you and me!

Destined Encounters

A hedgehog in sunglasses, what do you know?
He rolls with finesse, stealing every show.
With pigeons in bow ties and owls in hats,
The creatures unite, planning silly chats.

We meet on this road with our packs full of treats,
Sharing sandwiches, cakes, and some smelly old beets.
Laughter erupts as our stories unfold,
One's about a bear, but it's not quite as bold.

A raccoon joined in, with a wink and a nod,
He said, "Don't worry, I'm not a bad fraud!"
His paws held a trinket, a shiny old spoon,
He waved it around like it's bright as the moon.

In this jolly parade, destinies weave,
With each chuckle and cheer, more we believe.
These chance encounters, they twist and they bend,
In laughter and fun, we connect and transcend!

Together We Traverse

Two llamas in shades, strutting down the lane,
One trips on a twig, sings, "Oh, what a pain!"
They bounce back in rhythm, hooves tapping with flair,
An impromptu tango in the wild, without care.

With snacks in our pockets, we march hand in hoof,
Jellybeans roll out, which are usually aloof.
We scoot and we scuffle, oh what's that we see?
A fox in a tutu, quite fancy and free!

"Care to join us?" the llamas did grin,
"Step right on up, let the fun now begin!"
With laughter galore, we prance through the glade,
Every hop and jump feels like a grand parade.

As twilight approaches, our giggles resound,
We twirl with the stars, dancing round and round.
Each step we take adds another delight,
Together, we traverse, into the night!

Chords of Connectivity

In a park jammed with critters, quite a sight to behold,
A cat with a banjo, playing brave and bold.
The raccoons clap hands, trying to keep time,
While the snails slide in, thinking it's prime.

A frog jumps on stage, with a small little leap,
Declares he's the star, caused quite a heap!
With a ribbit and wink, and a hat full of sass,
The laughter erupts while the coyotes amass.

Together they sing in a hilarious tune,
As fireflies dance, lighting up like a moon.
Every giggle and snicker, they strum in the night,
While squirrels throw acorns, just trying for height!

Through chords of connection, they share their delight,
In comical chaos, they all take flight.
So here's to the fun, in this whimsical jam,
With furry friends joining, we all say "Oh, yeah, fam!"

Weaving Threads of Journey

In a world where socks go missing,
I find my shoes just reminiscing.
Laces tangled in a playful dance,
Each step feels like a comic chance.

With backpacks filled with mismatched snacks,
We navigate through silly tracks.
A map drawn by a crayon hand,
Leading us to Giggle-Land.

Bus stops filled with friendly chatter,
Who knew that spilled juice could scatter?
A journey's end is never clear,
Just laughter shared and too much cheer.

Through funny faces, we ignite,
The lighter side of every flight.
We weave our tales with glee and jest,
In this mismatched trip, we are blessed.

Connected Destinies

Two peas in a pod, we roam the street,
With jellybeans our favorite treat.
A twist of fate, a wink, a nod,
In this funny fate, we walk abroad.

Through puddles splashed with giggles bright,
Our shoes are soaked, what a silly sight!
Chasing dreams on a bumpy ride,
In tangled paths, we chuckle wide.

Like shoelaces knotted in the rain,
We stumble, laugh, and rise again.
Shared adventures, a peanut brawl,
Connected destinies, we have a ball!

Through quirky turns our laughter flows,
Each misstep adds to the show.
In life's big circus, we take our chance,
With joy infectious, we laugh and prance.

The Lattice of Life

In the garden of quirks we plant,
With daisies that giggle and roses that chant.
A crooked line leads us astray,
Yet the laughter blooms bright every day.

We scrapbook memories, strange and bright,
This tapestry woven in pure delight.
Snuggling with bears that cannot bear,
Who said life's journey must be fair?

In a web where every thread spins wide,
Our footfalls collide, there's no place to hide.
Through silly stumbles and leaps of fate,
We celebrate the moments that are great.

Growing roots like tangled vines,
Sprouting joy through all the pines.
In this crazy weave, we find our fun,
In our lattice, laughter's never done.

Interwoven Dreams

Sipping cocoa on a wild breeze,
Frolicking through a forest of cheese.
Jumping puddles filled with delight,
In dreams interwoven, all feels right.

Mismatched shoes on curious feet,
With cotton candy as a treat.
Every twist adds to our play,
In this whimsical life, come what may.

Giggling clouds raining jolly drops,
Funky hats that spin and flop.
As we dance with the fireflies' gleam,
Our world unfolds like a funny dream.

Through stitches of laughter, we soar high,
No need for a map, just look to the sky.
With each shared giggle, we fly anew,
In our interwoven tales, there's always a clue.

Forged in Wander

We stumbled upon a wandering goat,
He showed us the way to a cheese boat.
With laughs in the air and smiles galore,
We followed that critter to find a sweet store.

A map made of crumbs led us astray,
The bread was so fresh it danced all day.
With giggles we chased every slice in sight,
Each roll had a joke that tickled our night.

We tripped over laughter, fell hard in glee,
Our feet found a rhythm like ants at a spree.
In every misstep, joy's spark would ignite,
Like fireflies scattered in warm summer night.

Hand in hand we juggled a parade,
A tap dance of fate we'd happily made.
Through cheese and through bread, we carved out a song,

In the land of the silly, we all did belong.

Unity in Motion

We gathered our feet and donned our best hats,
In a parade of the odd, surrounded by cats.
With a wobbly step, and a toast to the sky,
We spun round and round, oh me, oh my!

A knight rode a unicycle, juggled with flair,
While we cheered him on from the comfort of air.
We pitched our tent in a sea of bright socks,
Camping out here among chairs and rocks.

A conga line formed with a whimsical twist,
Every step was a giggle, no wiggle was missed.
We danced through the night, a wild, merry show,
In synchronized chaos, we all stole the glow.

With arms interlinked, we launched into space,
Our laughter a rocket, we'd win any race.
Who knew that our journey could hold such delight?
In unity's chaos, we glimmered so bright!

The Collective Trek

On a journey so quirky, we ventured as one,
With hats made of flowers, we basked in the sun.
We hummed to the beat of a silly old tune,
As ducks in top hats all danced to the moon.

With backpacks of giggles and pockets of cheer,
We marched through the fields, not a worry or fear.
A parade of odd socks was leading the way,
A fashion show starring the colors of play.

We fumbled in mud, covered head to toe,
Each slip made us burst into fits of a show.
From puddles to stumbles, we conquered each plight,
Together we laughed through the heart of the night.

In a huddle we whispered our dreams like a spell,
That magic would chase us, we'd follow it well.
Through winding and winding, our fun never waned,
United in laughter, our adventure sustained!

Pathways of Connection

We forged our own way with a dance and a spin,
On tracks made of muffins, adventures begin.
In a sea of confetti, we tumbled and twirled,
Each step was a giggle, the whole world unfurled.

With a cat on a leash and a laugh in our pack,
We set out to conquer the hero-less track.
A map drawn in crayons, no lines or straight edges,
Led us through laughter, and bumpy old ledges.

A grand game of hopscotch made bridges explode,
We leapt from one giggle to another, it flowed.
Through the chaos of cheer, we found our way smooth,
In the fun, we discovered the joy of our groove.

With balloons as our compass, we floated through skies,
On this quirky adventure, our hearts gave a rise.
Together we wandered, mismatched and bright,
In a world sewn with humor, we laughed through the night.

As One We Wander

In mismatched shoes, we roam the streets,
Chasing pigeons, where laughter meets.
A map drawn in crayon, what chaos ensues,
With giggles and snorts, we follow our clues.

Through puddles we leap, like clumsy young deer,
Splashing each other, no sign of fear.
The sun might be blazing, but our minds are cool,
In our silly shenanigans, we find our own rule.

The Intersection of Hearts

Two paths converge where the ice cream man stops,
We barter our change for the newest lollipops.
With sticky fingers and giggles galore,
Every taste of adventure leaves us wanting more.

The traffic light dances, but we just delay,
Making up stories to pass the time away.
We argue on which way to head for some fries,
In the end, it's the friendship that makes us so wise.

Merging Ways

When I bring the snacks, we join in one feast,
While wild squirrels eye us, they think we're the least.
We hijack the trails with our quirky sweet songs,
Annoying the birds; they'll fly along!

Our footprints entwined, like spaghetti on plates,
We duel with shadows, and dance with fate.
There's strength in our laughter, a bond not so weak,
In the silly moments, it's friendship we seek.

The Compass of Companionship

We're lost in the woods with no hint of a clue,
But you've got a compass that points towards the stew!
With every wrong turn, more giggles arise,
A quest for the snacks becomes filled with surprise.

The squirrels become our advisory board,
As we navigate trouble with laughter and hoard.
The stars will align, or so we declare,
As long as you're here, I've got not a care.

The Harmony of Steps

In the dance of our two left feet,
We trip over cake, now that's a treat!
With mismatched socks and laughter loud,
We spin like tops, we're so very proud.

Around the corners, we giggle and glide,
Like ducks in rain, there's nowhere to hide.
Side by side, we make quite the pair,
A wobbly tune fills the air with flair.

Chasing our shadows under the sun,
In this game of life, we've already won!
With each little stumble, we find our groove,
It's clear our silliness makes us move.

So let's prance on this crooked lane,
Where joy is shared and laughter reigns.
Together we roam, you and I so free,
In the harmony of our hilarity.

An Intertwined Expedition

On this journey, oh what fun!
Who knew we'd need a map and a bun?
We take wrong turns, yet always cheer,
Every misstep brings us near!

With backpacks stuffed with snack and goo,
We hike past a llama, just me and you.
It spits at us, and we both burst out,
'Was that a greeting or just some doubt?'

Through muddy puddles and slippery trails,
We balance like clowns, wearing funny tails.
With giggles echoing from start to end,
In this wild escapade with my best friend!

So on we wander, maps askew,
Strange paths twist, that much is true.
But with you beside, I just can't lose,
In this intertwined adventure we choose.

The Arc of Adventure

A loop-de-loop trail leads us astray,
But who needs directions? We'll just play!
With snacks in hand, we take on the quest,
In search for the best, we're simply the best.

Through forests of whimsy, we bounce with glee,
Chasing a squirrel who's faster than we.
We'll make a grand map with crayons and cheer,
Who knew getting lost could be such a dear?

With each silly slip, we sing a new tune,
A pirouette here, a jig under the moon.
This arc of our journey, a funny delight,
With laughter as fuel, we soar through the night!

So let's sketch our tracks in bright neon flair,
For every misstep is a reason to share.
In the art of adventure, no frowns will we wear,
Just giggles and grins, we'll dance through the air!

Joined in Journey

Two pals on a bike, what a sight to behold,
With one on the pedals, the other feels bold.
We swerve and we weave, almost hit a tree,
But we just laugh it off, as happy as can be.

In puddles we splash, wearing mismatched shoes,
Each turn that we take, we find more to lose.
With antics and jokes, we're never alone,
On this path of mischief, we've brilliantly grown.

Under starlit skies, we chart our own fate,
With giggles and stories that we call great.
For every odd laugh and hop on one foot,
This journey together is one we imprint.

So here's to the ride, may it never end,
With you by my side, my lifelong friend.
In shared splendid chaos, our hearts sing true,
Joined in this journey, just me and you!

Bonded by the Sun

We trekked through clouds, so high and bright,
Accidentally tripped over a kite!
Laughter erupted, while we found our shoes,
Chasing shadows, we danced and refused.

With flip-flops squeaking on the sandy shore,
We stumbled and giggled, who could ask for more?
A sunscreen battle, it flew through the air,
Sunburned laughter — a perfect pair!

Finding treasures on the ocean's spine,
Shells that whispered, "This is divine!"
Each splash and tumble was nothing but fun,
What's a trip without a bit of a run?

As the day waned, with a sunset in tow,
We strung memories like beads in a row.
In the warmth of the sun, our hearts grow fat,
Who knew that traveling would include all that?

The Quilt of Our Travels

In the patchwork world where we took our flight,
Stitching together both day and night.
Crammed in a car, can you hear the tunes?
Giggling over snacks, counting the raccoons?

With maps upside down, we made quite the scene,
Wondering where all the tourists had been.
Each twist and turn was an unguided dream,
Until we camped near a marshmallow stream.

A blanket of laughter held us so tight,
Around the campfire, we danced with delight.
Mismatched stories, like patches, they shine,
As we hold up a cuppa and toast with a swine!

So here's to the quilt made of silly moments,
Sewn with great love and sweet endowments.
At each silly stop, we got close, we were bold,
Our travel tales wrapped us in laughter's fold!

Whirling Paths of Light

Around we spun, on a carousel ride,
Chasing the sun as our laughter did glide.
In fields of daisies, we rolled and we tumbled,
Tickling the earth, we just giggled, we fumbled.

Our feet were a blur, like leaves in the breeze,
Chasing fireflies, our hearts took a squeeze.
Through dappled woods where squirrels act wise,
We whispered secrets as the stars filled the skies.

With cupcakes devoured at a roadside stand,
We mapped out adventures, holding hands.
Every wrong turn led us to cheer,
Who knew that getting lost would bring us so near?

As the day faded, we danced in the glow,
Under moonlit skies where the soft breezes flow.
These whirling paths of the day we embrace,
With smiles that will leave a permanent trace!

Interlaced Journeys

On tangled trails, we made silly bets,
Swapping mismatched shoes, creating odd sets.
Through puddles of laughter, we splashed with glee,
No plan was too silly, oh come ride with me!

Guided by maps that were sketched in crayon,
Eating ice cream cones till the last drips were gone.
With every sweet bite, our spirits would rise,
Who knew that a road trip could yield such surprise?

Roaming the streets in our hats that were bright,
Requesting directions with pure delight.
We danced through the rain, in our mismatched attire,
Making stories that twinkled like stars in a choir.

So here's to the journeys where laughter aligns,
Interlaced moments like vintage designs.
The fun that we gathered, like gems on a string,
In this wacky adventure, we found our own zing!

Dual Trails

Two folks with maps that don't quite match,
One looking left, the other a scratch.
They giggle and wander, a comical sight,
In search of a burger, they just might bite!

They follow a squirrel—oh, what a chase!
Getting lost in giggles, losing all grace.
With each little turn, another snack found,
A perfect duet—missteps abound!

Mosaics of Movement

A cat on a leash, what a wobbly sight,
He zigzags and weaves, oh, what pure delight!
A lady with ice cream and shoes that flip,
Step on toes while they both take a trip!

The pavement's a canvas, each step a dance,
Spilled drinks and laughter, what a weird chance.
Finding the rhythm in chaotic glee,
Their silly synchrony is all that they see!

Interwoven Voyages

A turtle and rabbit set off on a spree,
Who's winning the race? Neither, you see!
They stop for a picnic, munch snacks galore,
The finish line? They forgot what's in store!

With laughter and crumbs stuck right in their fur,
They travel together, a merry old blur.
The world's full of mischief, they're floating on air,
Taking each wrong turn with a wink and a flare!

Collective Routes

An old man with bingo and a pair of old shoes,
Wanders the forest, confused and amused.
He waves to the hikers, they smile and they cheer,
"Is this where we're going?" they laugh with no fear.

With paths overlapping, they giggle and share,
Mishaps and mayhem float up in the air.
A circus of travelers, a motley old crew,
In the end, it's the journey that ties them all true!

www.ingramcontent.com/pod-product-compliance
Lightning Source LLC
Chambersburg PA
CBHW060123230426
43661CB00003B/315